Animals All

Copyright © 1979, Grisewood and Dempsey

Library of Congress Number: 78-21029

    3 4 5 6 7 8 9 0

Printed in the United States of America.

Library of Congress Cataloging in Publication Data

Main entry under title:

   Animals all.

   SUMMARY: Includes pictures of a variety of animals
accompanied by poetic text.
   1.   Animals — Juvenile poetry.   [1.   Animals — Poetry.
2.   American poetry]   I.   Manley, Deborah.   II.   Thompson, George William,
1925-
PZ8.3.A5493   811'.5'4   78-21029
ISBN 0-8172-1309-0 lib. bdg.

Animals All

Edited by
Deborah Manley

Pictures by
George Thompson

RAINTREE CHILDRENS BOOKS
Milwaukee • Toronto • Melbourne • London

THE
SQUIRREL

THE SQUIRREL

Whisky, frisky,
Hippity hop,
Up he goes
To the tree top!

Whirly, twirly,
Round and round,
Down he scampers
To the ground.

Furly, curly
What a tail!
Tall as a feather
Broad as a sail!

Where's his supper?
In the shell,
Snappity, crackity,
Out it fell!

Author Unknown

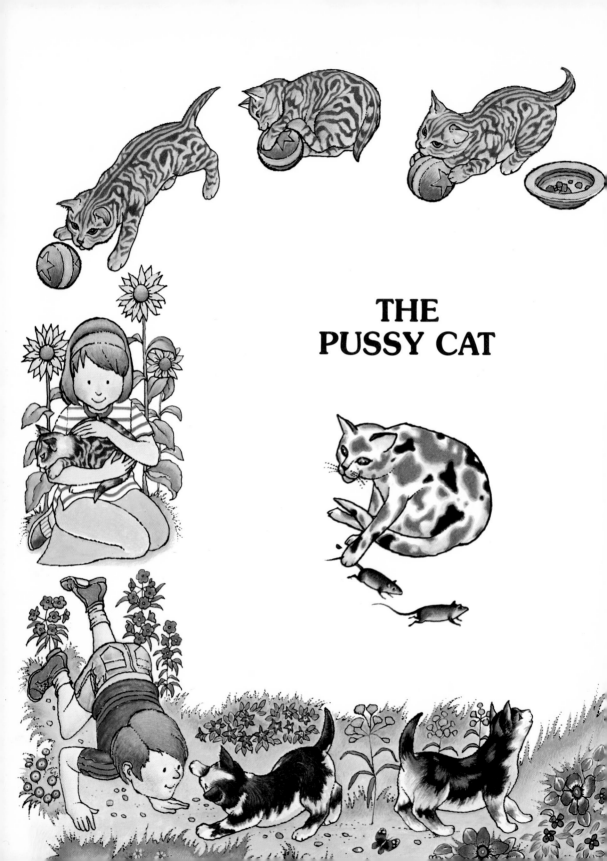

THE
PUSSY CAT

THE PUSSY CAT

I love little pussy,
　　Her coat is so warm,
And if I don't hurt her,
　　She'll do me no harm.

So I'll not pull her tail
　　Nor drive her away,
But pussy and I
　　Very gently will play.

She shall sit by my side
　　And I'll give her some food;
And pussy will love me
　　Because I am good.

Author Unknown

THE
CHICKENS

THE CHICKENS

Said the first little chicken,
  With a queer little squirm,
"I wish I could find
  A fat little worm!"

Said the next little chicken,
  With an odd little shrug:
"I wish I could find
  A fat little bug!"

Said the third little chicken,
  With a small sigh of grief:
"I wish I could find
  A green little leaf!"

Said the fourth little chicken,
  With a faint little moan:
"I wish I could find
  A wee gravel stone!"

"Now see here!" said the mother,
  From the green garden patch,
"If you want any breakfast,
  Just come here and scratch!"

Author Unknown

THE
FRIENDLY COW

THE FRIENDLY COW

The friendly cow all red and white,
I love with all my heart:
She gives me cream with all her might,
To eat with apple tart.

She wanders lowing here and there,
And yet she cannot stray,
All in the pleasant open air,
The pleasant light of day.

And blown by all the winds that pass
And wet with all the showers
She walks along the meadow grass
And eats the meadow flowers.

Robert Louis Stevenson

FURRY BEAR

If I were a bear,
　　And a big bear too,
I shouldn't much care
　　If it froze or snew;
I shouldn't much mind
　　If it snowed or friz —
I'd be all fur-lined
　　With a coat like his!

For I'd have fur boots and a brown fur wrap,
And brown fur knickers and a big fur cap.
I'd have a fur muffle-ruff to cover my jaws,
And brown fur mittens on my big brown paws.
With a big brown furry-down up to my head,
I'd sleep all winter in a big fur bed.

A. A. Milne

THE
SECRET

THE SECRET

We have a secret, just we three,
The robin, and I, and the sweet cherry-tree;
The bird told the tree, and the tree told me,
And nobody knows it but just us three.

But of course the robin knows it best,
Because he built the — I shan't tell the rest;
And laid the four little — something in it—
I'm afraid I shall tell it every minute.

But if the tree and the robin don't peep,
I'll try my best the secret to keep;
Though I know when the little birds fly about
Then the whole secret will be out.

Author Unknown

WHEN YOU SEE MAGPIES

One for sorrow,
Two for joy,
Three for a girl,
Four for a boy,
Five for silver.
Six for gold,
Seven for a secret
That is never to be told.

Author Unknown

LITTLE BIRD

Once I saw a little bird
   Come hop, hop, hop,
And I cried, "Little bird,
   Will you stop, stop, stop."

I was going to the window
To say, "How do you do?"
But he shook his little tail
And away he flew.

Author Unknown

THE ELEPHANT

When people call this beast to mind
They marvel more and more
At such a little tail behind,
So large a trunk before.

Hilaire Belloc

MICE

I think mice
Are rather nice.
    Their tails are long,
    Their faces small,
    They haven't any
    Chins at all.
    Their ears are pink,
    Their teeth are white,
    They run about
    The house at night.

20

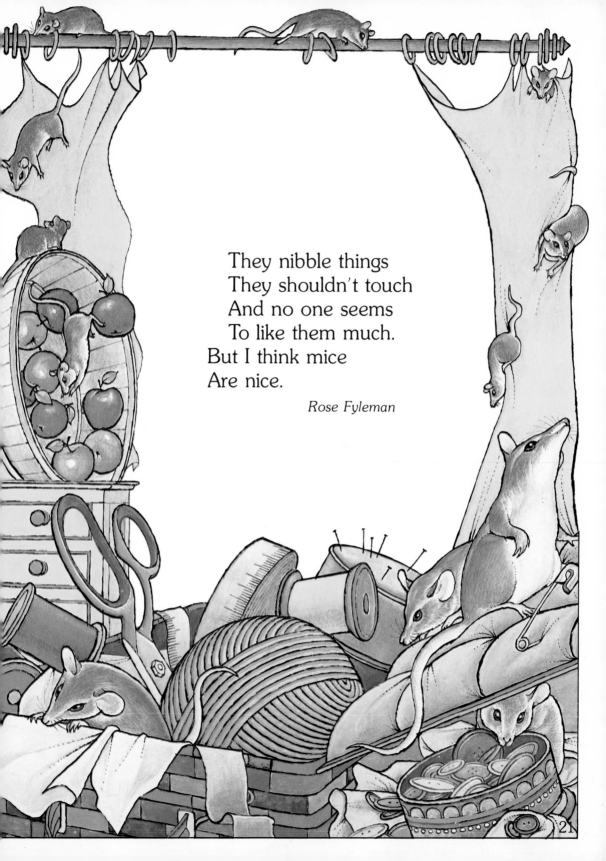

They nibble things
They shouldn't touch
And no one seems
To like them much.
But I think mice
Are nice.

Rose Fyleman

21

I SPEAK,
I SAY,
I TALK

Cats purr.
Lions roar.
Owls hoot.
Bears snore.
Crickets creak.
Mice squeak.
Sheep baa.
But I SPEAK!

Monkeys chatter.
Cows moo.
Ducks quack.
Doves coo.
Pigs squeal.
Horses neigh.
Chickens cluck.
I SAY!

Flies hum.
Dogs howl.
Bats screech.
Coyotes howl.
Frogs croak.
Parrots squawk.
Bees buzz.
But I TALK!

Arnold L. Shapiro

THE TIRED CATERPILLAR

A tired caterpillar went to sleep one day
In a snug little cradle of silken gray.
And he said, as he softly curled up in his nest,
"Oh, crawling was pleasant, but rest is best."

He slept through the winter long and cold,
All tightly up in his blanket rolled,
And at last he awoke on a warm spring day
To find that winter had gone away.

He awoke to find he had golden wings,
And no longer need crawl over sticks and things.
"Oh, the earth is nice," said the glad butterfly,
"But the sky is best, when we learn to fly!"

Author Unknown

GOODBYE

Leaves are skipping round the door,
Blackberries are ripe once more;
Acorns in the long grass lie;
Swallow, swallow, say goodbye!

Mouse and mole and rabbit sleep
In their snug holes dry and deep;
Frost is on the field today.
Swallow, swallow, fly away!

Soon great winds will roar and shout,
Tossing the brown leaves about;
Soon will fly the whirling snow;
Swallow, swallow, off you go!

But when hawthorn buds unfold
And the primrose spreads her gold,
And violets are in the lane,
Swallow, swallow, come again!

Marjorie Stannard

OLD NOAH'S ARK

OLD NOAH'S ARK

Old Noah once he built an ark,
And patched it up with hickory bark.
He anchored it to a great big rock,
And then he began to load his stock.
The animals went in one by one,
The elephant chewing a carroway bun.
The animals went in two by two,
The crocodile and the kangaroo.
The animals went in three by three,
The tall giraffe and the tiny flea,
The animals went in four by four,
The hippopotamus stuck in the door.
The animals went in five by five,
The bees mistook the bear for a hive.
The animals went in six by six,
The monkey was up to his usual tricks.
The animals went in seven by seven,
Said the ant to the elephant, "Who're ye shov'n?"
The animals went in eight by eight,
Some were early and some were late.
The animals went in nine by nine,
They all formed fours and marched in a line.
The animals went in ten by ten,
If you want any more, you can read it again.

Folk Rhyme

This will help you with the Word Review.

a	a as in **cat**
ā	a as in **able**
ä	a as in **father**
e	e as in **bend**
ē	e as in **me**
i	i as in **in**
ī	i as in **ice**
o	o as in **top**
ō	o as in **old**
ô	o as in **cloth**
oo	oo as in **good**
o͞o	oo as in **tool**
oi	oi as in **oil**
ou	ou as in **out**
u	u as in **up**
ur	ur as in **fur**
yo͞o	u as in **use**
ə	a as in **again**
ch	ch as in **such**
ng	ng as in **sing**
sh	sh as in **shell**
th	th as in **three**
<u>th</u>	th as in **that**

Word Review

Here are some words from *Animals All.* Practice saying each word out loud. See if you can find them in the book.

butterfly (but′ ər flī′)
caterpillar (kat′ ər pil′ ər)
coyote (kī ō′ tē)
cricket (krik′ it)
crocodile (krok′ ə dīl′)
dove (duv)
flea (flē)
giraffe (jə raf′)
hippopotamus (hip′ ə pot′ ə məs)
kangaroo (kang′ gə roo′)
magpie (mag′ pī)
mice (mīs)
mole (mōl)
parrot (par′ ət)
robin (rob′ in)

We wish to acknowledge with thanks the following for use of the poems in this book: Methuen Children's Books for the poem *Furry Bear* from *Now We Are Six;* Gerald Duckworth & Co. Limited for *The Elephant* from *Bad Child's Book of Beasts;* The Society of Authors as the literary representative of the Estate of Rose Fyleman for the poem *Mice;* Field Enterprises Educational Corporation for *I Speak, I Say, I Talk* from Volume 1, *Childcraft — How and Why Library;* Marjorie Stannard for *Goodbye.*